ROCK CLASSICS

CONTENTS

2 Aqualung JETHRO TULL

4 Behind Blue Eyes THE WHO

6 Crazy Train OZZY OSBOURNE

8 Fly Like an Eagle STEVE MILLER BAND

10 Free Bird LYNYRD SKYNYRD

12 Hey Jude THE BEATLES

14 Into the Great Wide Open TOM PETTY

16 Low Rider WAR

18 Maggie May ROD STEWART

20 Oye Como Va SANTANA

22 Proud Mary CREEDENCE CLEARWATER REVIVAL

24 Smoke on the Water DEEP PURPLE

26 Start Me Up THE ROLLING STONES

28 We Will Rock You QUEEN

30 You Really Got Me VAN HALEN

Arrangements by Adam Perlmutter

ISBN 978-1-4234-3560-0

HAL•LEONARD®
CORPORATION
7777 W. BLUEMOUND RD. P.O. BOX 13819 MILWAUKEE, WI 53213

Visit Hal Leonard Online at
www.halleonard.com

AQUALUNG

Music by Ian Anderson
Lyrics by Jennie Anderson

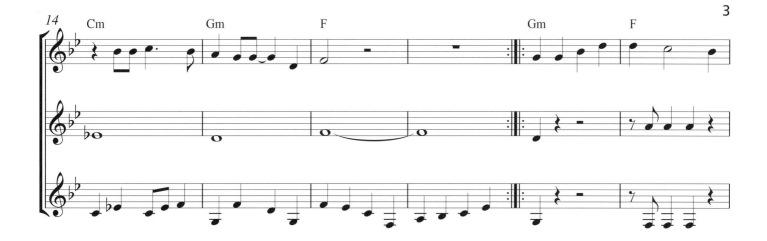

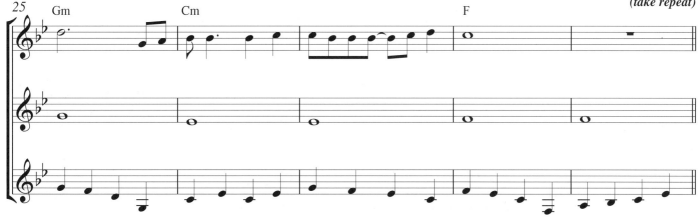

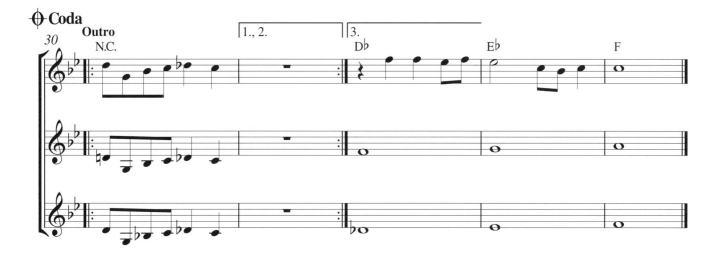

BEHIND BLUE EYES

Words and Music by Pete Townshend

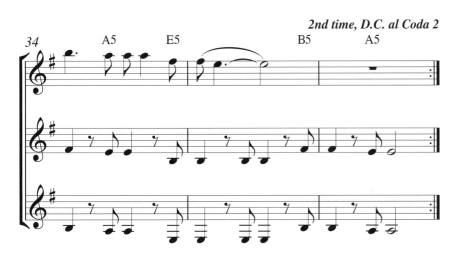

CRAZY TRAIN

Words and Music by Ozzy Osbourne, Randy Rhoads and Bob Daisley

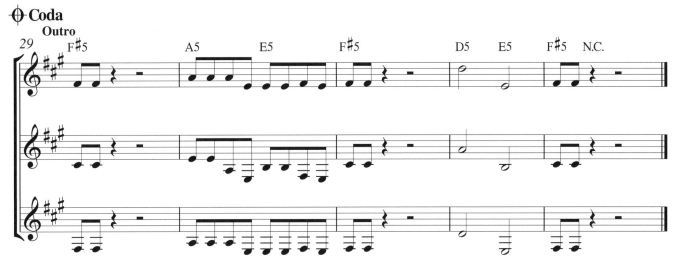

FLY LIKE AN EAGLE

Words and Music by Steve Miller

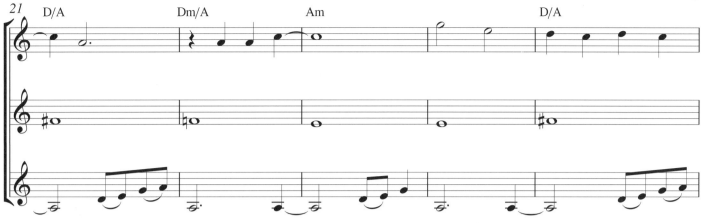

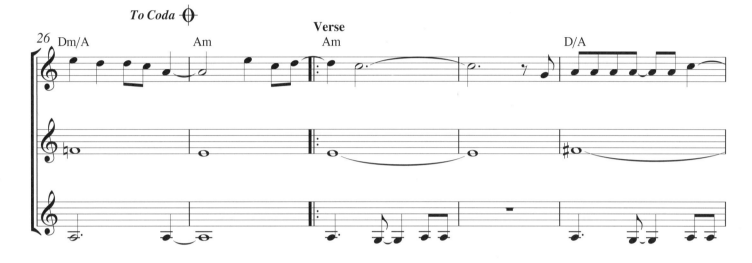

FREE BIRD

Words and Music by Allen Collins and Ronnie Van Zant

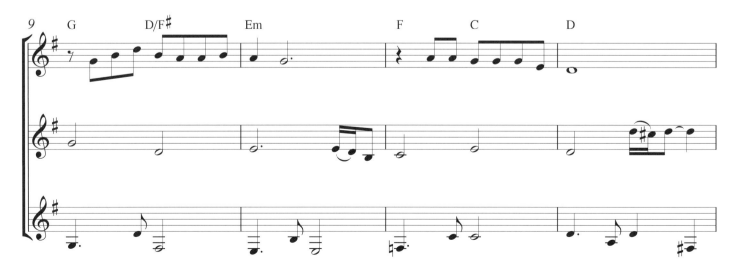

HEY JUDE

Words and Music by John Lennon and Paul McCartney

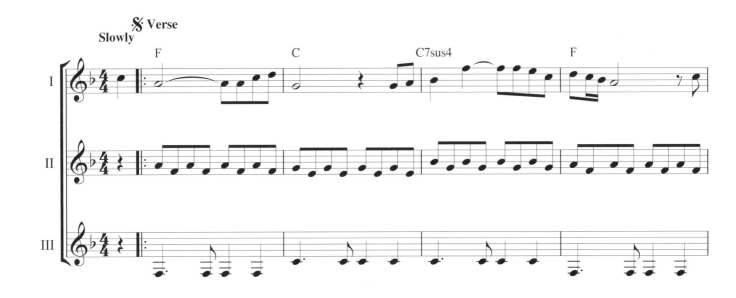

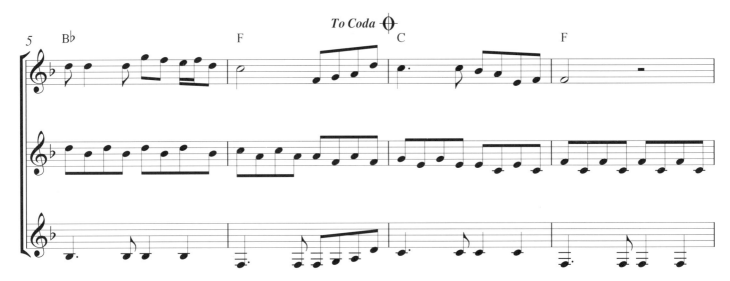

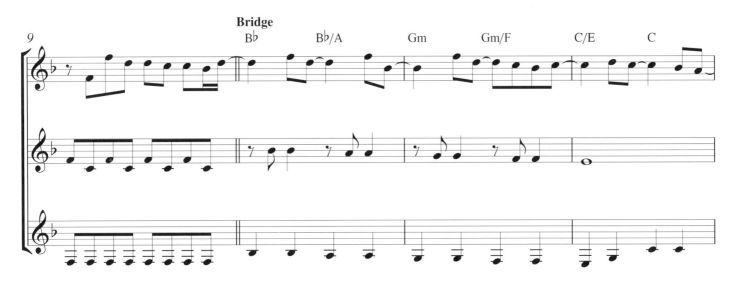

2nd time, D.S. al Coda

Coda

Outro

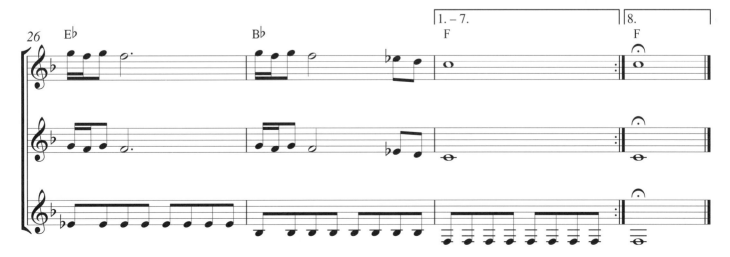

INTO THE GREAT WIDE OPEN

Words and Music by Tom Petty and Jeff Lynne

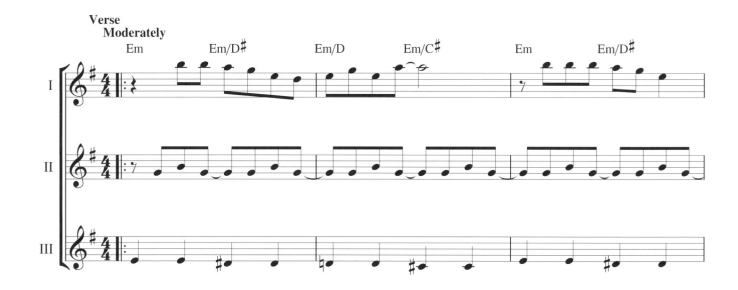

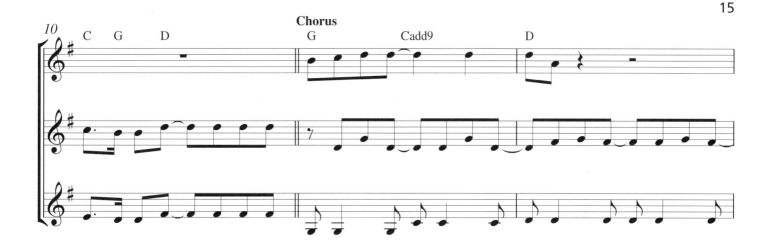

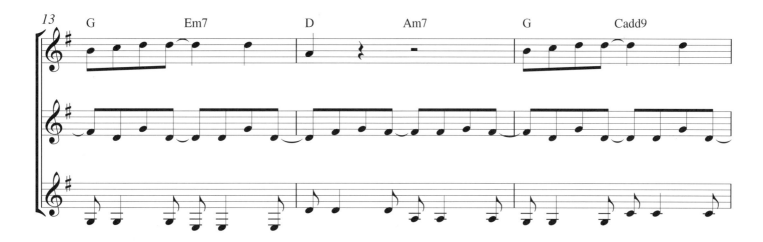

Chorus

To Coda ⊕

D.C. al Coda
(take repeat)

⊕ Coda

LOW RIDER

Words and Music by Sylvester Allen, Harold R. Brown, Morris Dickerson,
Jerry Goldstein, Leroy Jordan, Lee Oskar, Charles W. Miller and Howard Scott

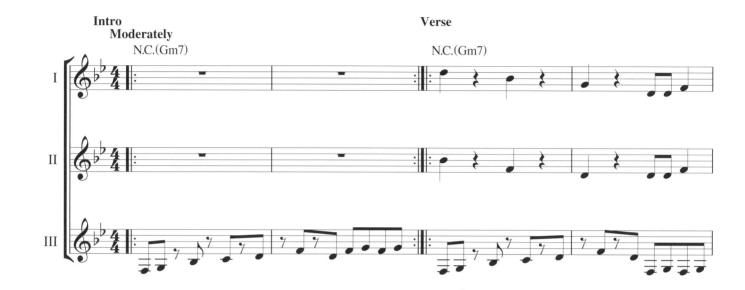

Outro

N.C.(Gm7)

Play 4 times

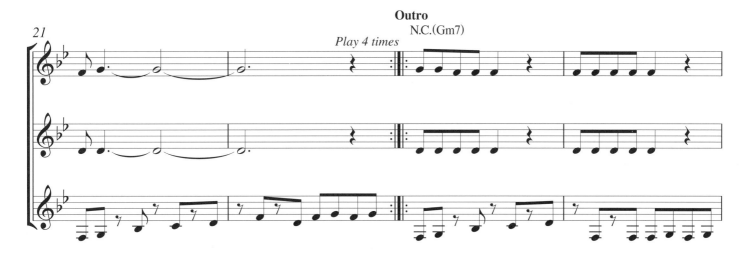

N.C.

Play 4 times

MAGGIE MAY

Words and Music by Rod Stewart and Martin Quittenton

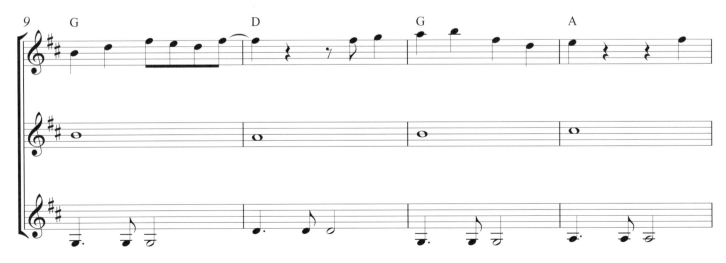

Chorus

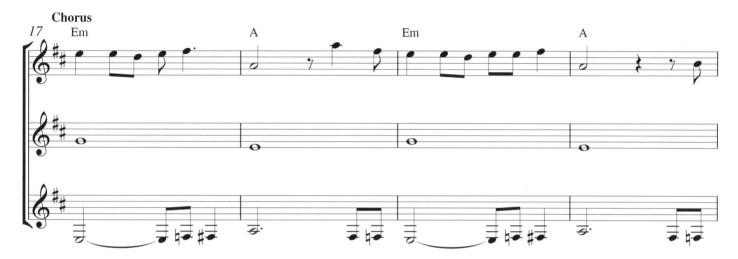

Outro

OYE COMO VA

Words and Music by Tito Puente

Intro
Moderately

Chorus   **Guitar Solo**

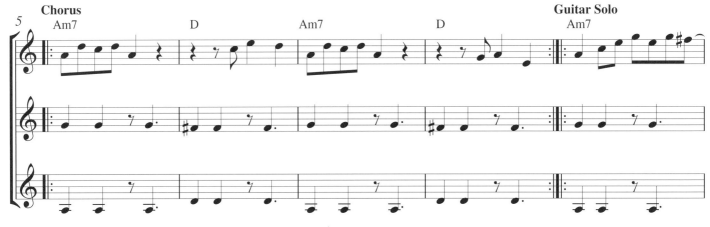

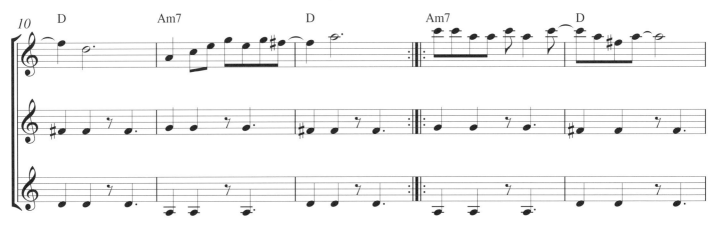

Interlude

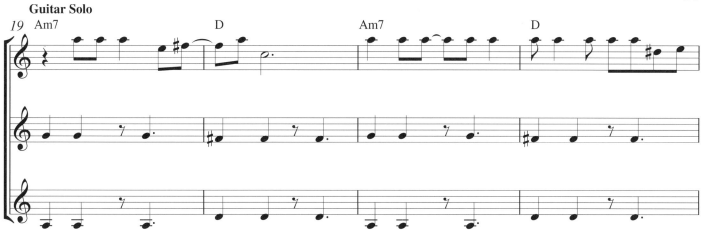

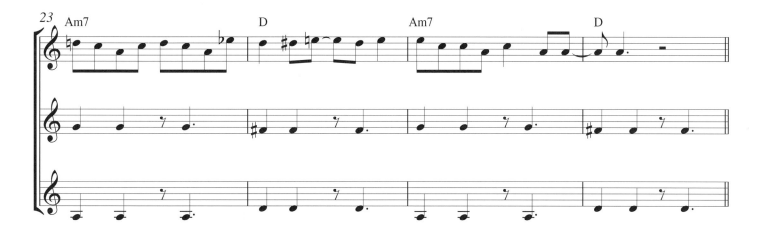

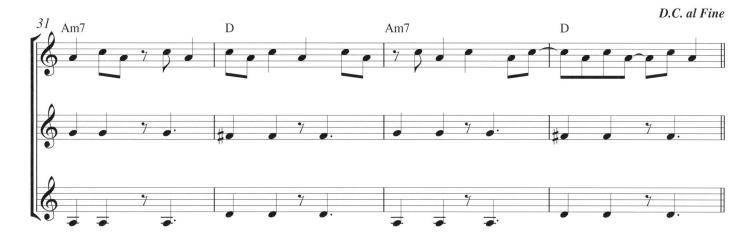

PROUD MARY
Words and Music by John Fogerty

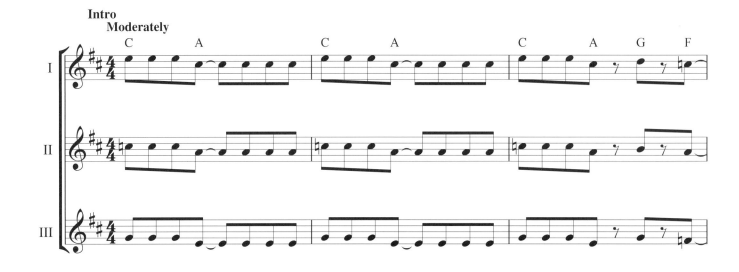

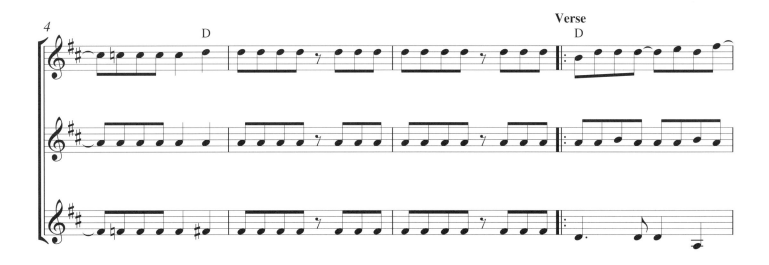

Pre-Chorus

Chorus

To Coda ⊕
2nd time, D.C. al Coda

⊕ Coda

SMOKE ON THE WATER

Words and Music by Ritchie Blackmore, Ian Gillan, Roger Glover, Jon Lord and Ian Paice

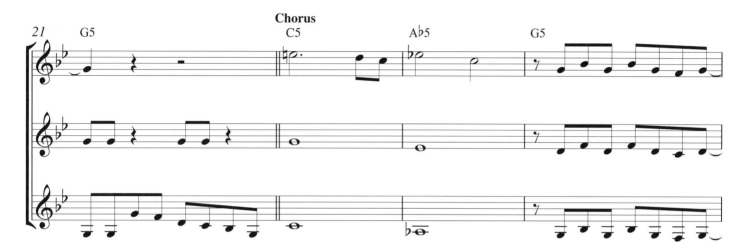

Chorus

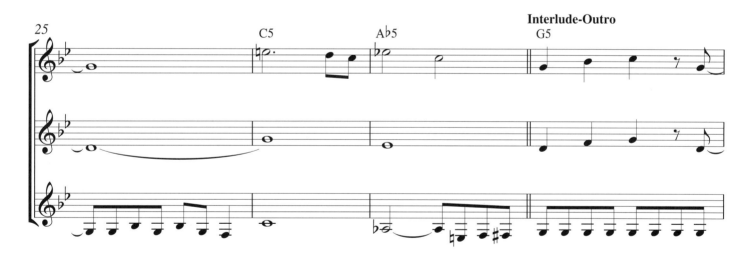

Interlude-Outro

START ME UP
Words and Music by Mick Jagger and Keith Richards

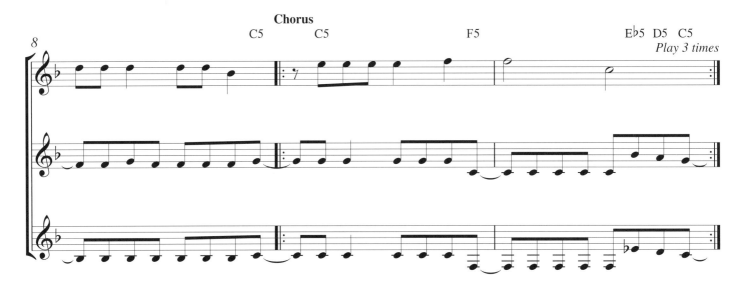

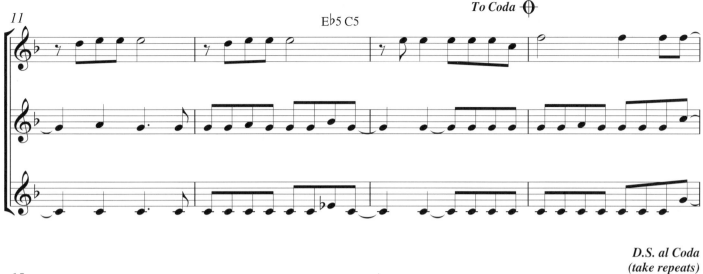

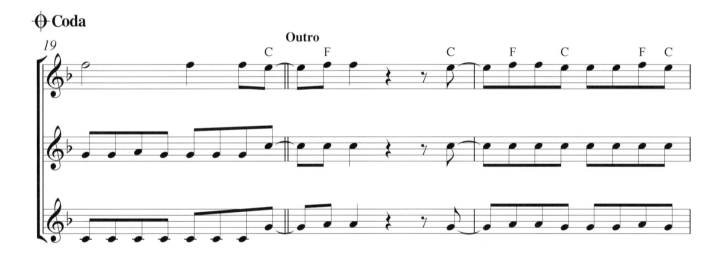

WE WILL ROCK YOU

Words and Music by Brian May

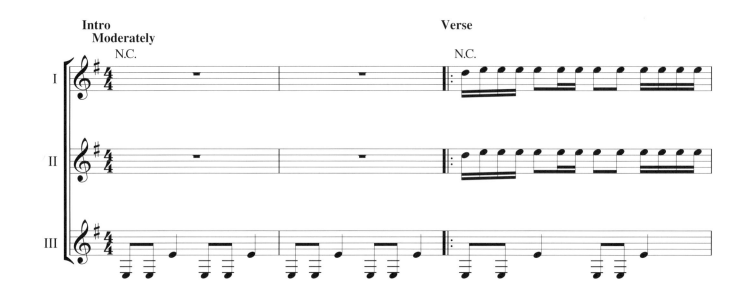

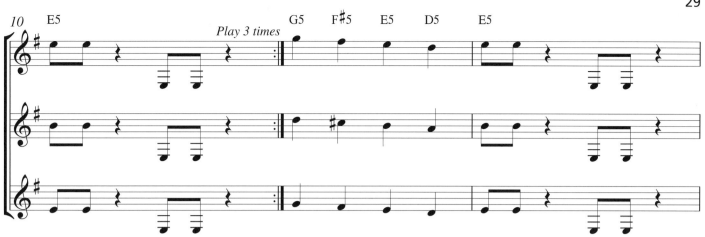

YOU REALLY GOT ME

Words and Music by Ray Davies

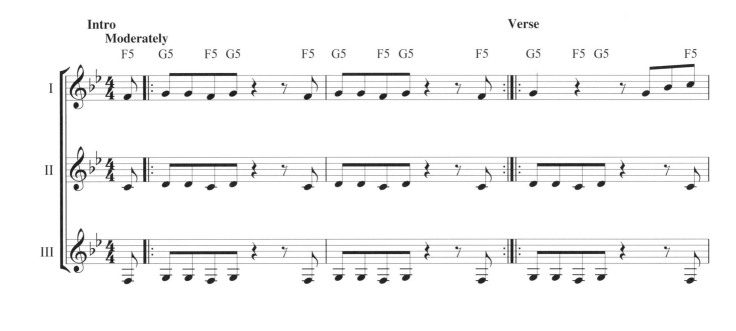

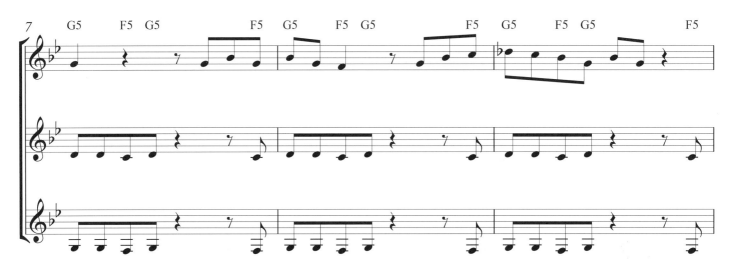

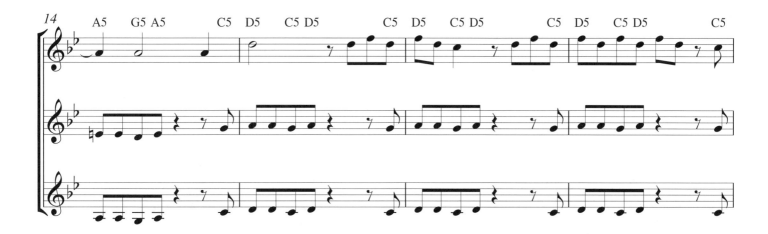

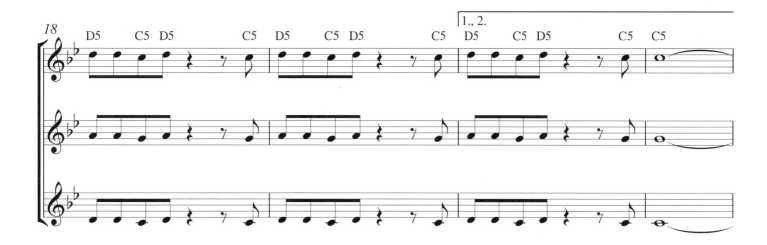

ESSENTIAL ELEMENTS FOR GUITAR

Essential Elements Comprehensive Guitar Method

Take your guitar teaching to a new level! With popular songs in a variety of styles, and quality demonstration and backing tracks on the accompanying online audio, *Essential Elements for Guitar* is a staple of guitar teachers' instruction – and helps beginning guitar students off to a great start. This method was designed to meet the National Standards for Music Education, with features such as cross-curricular activities, quizzes, multicultural songs, basic improvisation and more.

BOOK 1

by Will Schmid and Bob Morris

Concepts covered in Book 1 include: getting started; basic music theory; guitar chords; notes on each string; music history; ensemble playing; performance spotlights; and much more! Songs include: Dust in the Wind • Eleanor Rigby • Every Breath You Take • Hey Jude • Hound Dog • Let It Be • Ode to Joy • Rock Around the Clock • Stand by Me • • Sweet Home Chicago • This Land Is Your Land • You Really Got Me • more!

00862639 Book/Online Audio $17.99
00001173 Book Only $10.99

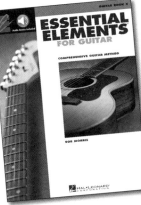

BOOK 2

by Bob Morris

Concepts taught in Book 2 include: playing melodically in positions up the neck; movable chord shapes up the neck; scales and extended chords in different keys; fingerpicking and pick style; improvisation in positions up the neck; and more! Songs include: Auld Lang Syne • Crazy Train • Folsom Prison Blues • La Bamba • Landslide • Nutcracker Suite • Sweet Home Alabama • Your Song • and more.

00865010 Book/Online Audio $17.99
00120873 Book Only $10.99

Essential Elements Guitar Ensembles

The songs in the Essential Elements Guitar Ensemble series are playable by three or more guitars. Each arrangement features the melody, a harmony part, and bass line in standard notation along with chord symbols. For groups with more than three or four guitars, the parts can be doubled. This series is perfect for classroom guitar ensembles or other group guitar settings.

Mid-Beginner Level

EASY POP SONGS
00865011/$10.99

CHRISTMAS CLASSICS
00865015/$9.99

CHRISTMAS SONGS
00001136/$10.99

Late Beginner Level

CLASSICAL THEMES
00865005/$9.99

POP HITS
00001128/$10.99

ROCK CLASSICS
00865001/$9.99

TURBO ROCK
00001076/$9.95

Early Intermediate Level

J.S. BACH
00123103/$9.99

THE BEATLES
00172237/$9.99

CHRISTMAS FAVORITES
00128600/$9.99

DISNEY SONGS
00865014/$12.99

IRISH JIGS & REELS
00131525/$9.99

JAZZ BALLADS
00865002/$9.99

MULTICULTURAL SONGS
00160142/$9.99

POPULAR SONGS
00241053/$9.99

TOP SONGS 2010-2019
00295218/$9.99

Mid-Intermediate Level

THE BEATLES
00865008/$14.99

BLUES CRUISE
00000470/$9.95

BOSSA NOVA
00865006/$12.99

CHRISTMAS CLASSICS
00865015/$9.99

DUKE ELLINGTON
00865009/$9.99

GREAT THEMES
00865012/$10.99

JIMI HENDRIX
00865013/$9.99

JAZZ STANDARDS
00865007/$12.99

MYSTERIOSO
00000471/$9.95

ROCK HITS
00865017/$9.99

ROCK INSTRUMENTALS
00123102/$9.99

TOP HITS
00130606/$9.99

Late Intermediate to Advanced Level

JAZZ CLASSICS
00865016/$9.99

Essential Elements Guitar Songs

The [...] books in the Essential Elements Guitar Songs series feature popular songs selected for the practice of specific guitar chord types. Each book includes eight songs and a CD with fantastic sounding play-along tracks. Practice at any tempo with the included Amazing Slow Downer software!

BARRE CHORD ROCK
00001137 Late-Beginner Level $12.99

POWER CHORD ROCK
00001139 Mid-Beginner Level $15.99

More Resources

DAILY GUITAR WARM-UPS
by Tom Kolb
Mid-Beginner to Late Intermediate
00865004 Book/Online Audio $14.99

GUITAR FLASH CARDS
96 Cards for Beginning Guitar
00865000...$10.99

Prices, contents, and availability subject to change without notice.

HAL•LEONARD®
www.halleonard.com